I0161205

In the Middle of
BeLIEve
There's a Lie

By Dudley (CHRIS) Christian

A

Pause For Poetry©

Publication

Acknowledgement:

Special thanks to my wife, Marilyn Christian for compiling, organizing and finalizing the books of my collections. Her photographic and editing skills were vital to all of my works.

ISBN: 978-0-9916853-1-8

First Edition April 2013
Revised Edition June 2017

Dudley (Chris) Christian founded and hosted the first and only "PAUSE FOR POETRY" show dedicated solely to the introduction of new and unknown poets and their works. This TV series ran from 1974 to 1985.

Cover: Designed by Dudley and Marilyn Christian

An Opening Word by the author....

Often people ask:

"How do you write and do you have to often rewrite your material?"

I have long summed up my answer to the above with the following:

"A Word, the written word, small purveyor of a thought, so like a thought, once thought, cannot be recalled, so too, a word once writ, should need NOT be re-written, for with such license, we would but change ... the very substance of the thought."

... DNC © 1970

* *

Table of Contents

For permission to use any of my lyrics with your music:

<u>Contact Information:</u>

Dudley (Chris) Christian

23848 113 B Avenue

Maple Ridge, BC Canada V2W 1V3

Email: dnc@telus.net

Dear Reader:

A-ways back, back beyond the early 1960s I wrote some rhymed lyrics for a few friends of my father, who used them for playing in their home bands. As time went on, I wrote more but didn't even think about putting these in a booklet or having any means of documenting their ownership. A few years later a shipmate of mine looked at and became interested in my few saved works. It was now in the end part of 1961 when I started haphazardly keeping a little book (attempting to keep a record) of some of my song lyrics, song poems, song ballads and even a few thoughts or ideas to be useable in movies or as concert fillers. I do NOT sing myself and as such never had the training to put my words to music vocally. Still my collections grew...

Thus to interested and/or musical friends:
"FOR YOU"...

Explore through these lyrics and see if you find something you would be willing to take a second long look at, with the hope or thought of being able to use it in your jam session or musicale. I do request that if you wish to use these lyrics, contact me (see previous page for contact information).

I'll Wait Forever For You

I'll wait forever for you
Out on the ocean so blue
For I know dreams do come true
So I'll wait forever for you

Calm seas or rough rolling waves
Dark nights or fog shrouded days
Here alone the seas I shall sail
As I wait forever for you.

I'll wait forever for you
I'll love you honest and true
My life yours as you will to do
While I wait forever for you.

I'll wait forever for you
Thru night dreams, fantasies too
'Til my life can be spent with you
Then I'll live forever with you.

Dr. Salve (Calypso Poem)

I've been paying very close attention
To an old Doctor friend of mine
Yes I've been paying close attention
An' ah sure he done it right this time
He's been very busy, busy that's for sure
Giving peoples prescriptions
To take to he own drug store
If it's headache, heartache, belly or backache
Or whatever ache the patient have
Is not anything like pill, drink, penicillin
The doctor only prescribing Salve

CHORUS:

Salve -- Salve -- Old Man Dr. Salve
Is the name he get from he patients
He don't have no understanding
'Bout the ailments they all having
But only recommending -- daily Salving
Salve -- Salve -- Old Man Dr. Salve

Now someplaces have started to wonder
Just how long this doctor will last
They say they 'fraid for the doctor
'Cause he applies the medicine so fast

Not another doctor,

Intern, nurse or person

Will he allow to apply he prescription

If you live a yard, a block or a mile

When you need salving

No matter where you living

Dr. Salve's by your side with a smile

CHORUS

So the Government decide to take action

By getting a drug specialist

They said they must protect

The doctor condition

Before they lose such a great salvist

Then the United Nation send their best

A lady certified in every wonder medicine

She take a fake test

Now she too can't resist

The sweet feelings of a daily Salving.

CHORUS

1962

Come On Baby Won'tcha Go My Way

CHORUS: *"Come on baby won'tcha go my way*
You know I'll love you 'til my dying day
And if I'm first to make it home
I'll send ya someone so you won't be 'lone"

Since I was just about three or four
I had a great fear about being alone
'Til my grandpappy would call and say
Come on baby won'tcha go my way ....
CHORUS

When grandpa died I was only five
Feeling let down me an' only child
But Daddy came home from war that day
And held me closely and softly said ....
CHORUS twice

I grew up fast and filled out good
At eighteen years a rose of womanhood
But I cried alone when Dad passed away
Feeling so empty 'til I heard you say ....
CHORUS

Now for all my years I was ne'er alone
But it's my time to travel home
So hold me close Darling as I say
You won't be lonely as I go my way ....
CHORUS twice and fade out

1977

I Go Back Into My Memories

I go back into my memories
To the ages of a past life
When my free and happy living I recall ---
Where the ladies all come calling

And my life 'twas never empty
As the sounds of laughter echoed o'er it all ---
Then I thought I'd be manly
And take a wife just for me

One whom with my future I could spend ---
Now my days are cold and empty
And my nights are long and lonely
As I pray somehow, someday it will end ---

CHORUS: *Oh my lonely lonely heart's in prison*
Where the walls are formed into a ring
Where the warden is the soft voice of a loved one
And the sentence is forever unending

I have done no crime in living I am certain
I had thought ever happy I could be
I had wanted only to make others happy
Now alas I want only -- to be free
CHORUS

A Green Christmas

(to the tune of "I'm Dreaming of a White Christmas")

I'm remembering a green Christmas

Just like the ones I always knew

Where seashells glistened

While children listened

To salt waves on shores where once I grew

===============

I'm remembering a green Christmas

Where by the moonlight cards I'd read

May your days all be sunny as seen

And may all your Christmases be green

===============

I'm remembering a green Christmas

Just like the ones I used to know

Where Mommy and Daddy

Sis, Brothers and Grannie

Loving family with faces aglow

===============

I'm remembering a green Christmas

Just like the ones I've always seen

And if this winter goes away

I'll return to those shores someday

And our Christmases will all again be green...

Days Before Xmas

(to the tune of "It Was The Night Before Christmas")

'Twas yet days before Christmas

But all thru our town

The feelings of yuletime

'Twas spreading around

The trees with icicles cold were all hung

On bare empty branches

Now the leaves had all gone

The grass green ungrowing

Like a carpet it lay

Suspended in beauty

Awaiting the Spring day

The children from school

All did merrily run

Awaiting the coming

Of the fat jolly one

Inside all the houses

In reds golds and whites

Decorations on green trees

Reflected the lights

The little brothers and sisters

Answered soft with such care

Each other as if guarding

What some other might hear
While the tots so wide-eyed
Stared impatient each day
As Mommy assured them
Santa is on his way
So we took this Yuletime
To stop by to see you
Remindful we'll always
Need friends warm and true
To wish you the best
For the whole coming year
And a Merry Merry Christmas to one
And all from all of us here.........

Too Many Times

Too many times, too many times
I've waited for you
Too many times, too many times
I've been lonely too
I know that you dear
Will never be just mine
For I've had to wait dear
Too, too, too many times
Too many times, too many times

I've cried all alone

Too many times, too many times

Wished you were my own

My poor heart tells me

That a new love you'll find

And I'll stay here lonely

Like too many times

Too many times, too many times

Alone with my tears

Too many times, too many times

Wishing that you were here

Tho I am waiting

I know I'll ne'er find

Fulfillment in you love

It's been too many times

Too many times, too many times

Just too many times

Why do you torture

This weary heart of mine

You could make me happy

If your love I could find

'Stead of waiting here lonely

Too many times

I'm Paying My Debt To Society

CHORUS:
.......*I'm paying my debt to society*
Watching the long years roll by
I'm paying my debt to society
But friend -- you're more prisoner than I........

My debt it was made from wrongdoing
I gambled in life's game and lost
My justice 'twas dealt to me fairly
My long prison term is the cost
Yet you walk on free and unseeing
Unmindful of all that you own
You're wasting your years intentionally
And too late you'll find them all gone.
CHORUS

I've lived as I wanted full and free
Ne'er regretful am I of that time
For my quest it was mine for fulfilling
Tho my quest to the law was a crime

You live doing what you don't want to
Obedient you to all that they say
Caging insides you your true desires
Shuffled ever along on your way

You're told when to work, sleep and play
You're shown what to wear, where to go
You learn what they choose for your teaching
With no whip still you're bent by the blow
CHORUS

In years soon again it'll be over
My debt will be paid and I'm free
You will work on your sentence unending
Surely more of a prisoner than me
When time comes to us for a reckoning
Regrets of a waste past you'll know
But tho I may be scorned for my actions
Deep within a true peace there shall glow
My quest has been filled to its fullest
And more than that man cannot attain

So look not upon me with pity
Had I life to relive I'd do it again
No harm have I caused to one person
All my crimes were but material gains
Same as your daily toiling unhappy
I achieved mine with so much less pain
Yes I'm paying my debt to society
Watching the long years roll by
I'm paying my debt to society
But I'll venture you're not contented as I.

Silvered Snowflakes Are Falling

(to the tune of "Brahms Lullaby")

Silvered snowflakes are falling
From the cold winter skies
Far away in the Northland
Hear the sleigh bells arrive
There's a toy laden man
With a team of Reindeer
Comes again loud the chime
It's the time of good cheer.

CHORUS: **Winter snows soft and white**
Fall thru daytime and night
Making soft fluffy trail
O'er which Santa can hail

See the soft winter's snow
On the mountains and trees
While snug in their beds
Dream the children of these
Dolls and guns, toys and wheels
Train sets and snowfields
Sleigh rides in the park
Spacemen glows in the dark.

Christmas time's drawing nigh

Hear the sleigh bells on high

Christmas time's drawing nigh

Hear the sleigh bells on high.

Christmas time's drawing nigh

Hear the sleigh bells on high.

Christmas time's drawing nigh

<u>If Your Love Is True Like Mine</u>

Is the moon too soft to caress thee

Are the stars too far to care

Is the wind too sweet to blow on your cheek

Not if your love is true like mine dear

Are the waves too soft to rock thee

Is the sun too warm to shine

Does rainbows come when day is done

Not if your love is true like mine dear

The songbird, could ne'er sing sweeter

The Owl could ne'er be more wise

Our love can't fail

My poor heart won't wail

Not if your love is true like mine dear

See The Waves Upon The Oceans Roar

(to the tune of "You Belong to Me")

See the waves upon the Oceans roar
Sending messages of love ashore
'Cross the harbour to one I adore
Where she waits for me.....

See the glitter of the city lights
Beaming like her smile into the night
Showing warmth like when she holds me tight
When she's in my arms....

Red the glow which shines across the sky
Planes like shooting stars above they fly
Each a tear which sparkled in her eye
When we kissed goodbye....

Take this message which I send to you
On the waves atop the ocean blue
Knowing that here "I Love You"
More than I can show....

See the city as it goes to bed
With its crown of lights around its head
For each light a tear each night I'll shed
'Til I'm back with you....

Grace's Theme

(to the tune of Lara's "Dr. Zhivago")

Somewhere

Your laughter once more will ring

And joy to my heart

The music of it 'twill bring

Sometimes a dream

Of days past your thoughts will hold

A dream of the past

More precious than finest gold

Someday

I'll hold you close like now

Someday

Tho I know not where or how

Till that day my sweet

You'll be in my heart so true

Till that day sweetheart

My dreams will be all of you

There Is A Street Called Loneliness

There is a street called Loneliness
Which runs near Empty Hollow
A suburb of a little town
Known as the Broken Heart

It's here that sorrow always lives
In front of All The Others
Which line the street of Loneliness
To keep the pieces all apart.

Near Sorrow lives Unforgetfulness
And next lives Tender Memories
A neighbour of The Times that's Been
Long Past and Now It's O'er

Two doors down lives Endless Dreams
Just before you turn the corner
Where 'What Has Been' and 'Cannot Mend'
Share houses side by side.

As you walk on the Gravel street
They'll look like cast off diamonds
Each one a heart that's crystallized
Before being cast down

Then too you'll see old 'Unmending'
A-sitting there by 'Lonely's' window
Reliving all that used to be
Before this little town was born.

Upon this street called Loneliness
You'll meet the Old and Aged
You'll also meet' The Infant' and 'The Young'
You'll see Both Sexes walking Dazed

Trying to find 'Who Brought them Hither'
With 'Nary a Word' or 'Answer Given'
Tho they question all they meet
Then at the last house of the street

If you care to look that far on
You'll see perhaps 'Familiar Scenes'
From 'The Love' that we once shared
The garden there I've planted it
With all our 'Flowered Memories'
In hopes one day I'll look and see
You -- walking up to here.

There is a street called Loneliness
Which runs near Empty Hollow
A suburb of a little town
Known as a Broken Heart
There is a street called Loneliness
Which runs near Empty Hollow...
A suburb of a little town
Known as a Broken Heart

Love Seen In Black And White

CHORUS:

I AM THE Black Man – The hard-working Black Man
That from Slaves grew up in this way
A child I of Afric – From across the deep waters
Where once free my peoples did stay
Please don't be frightened – I will not hurt you
No matter what others may say
Tho it's been said that our race should not mingle
I'm in need of some friendship today

There once was a charming white girl of great beauty
Who lived in her home by the woods
Afraid of the village where men once before
Had lied like she thought not they could
To think of the city beyond the small village
Brought renewed fear to her heart
For she'd heard the stories of all the Black Men there
Who ravaged the girls light or dark

Out of the city in his humble cottage
Sits a Black Man alone in the dark
His life is empty as he sits alone there
While the white girl ventures out in the park
All of a sudden a fear overcomes her
As she hears the voice of someone
She sees the Black Man beckoning to her
In fear she's too scared to run

Tho she couldn't tell why, she accepted this stranger
Placed her white hand upon his so black
And the fear she had felt at the sound of his speaking
Seemed so senseless when now she thought back
For she felt she could see deep within of the Black Man
And even then it crossed her mind
That she the white girl could fall for the Black Man
That he too would love her in time

Could the Black Man be lonely and seeking companion
To share life with in tenderness
Someone to trust him, love and protect him
As each day he fought prejudice
Then the Black Man spoke softly his voice shy and hurtful
With the pains of his life clearly there
Tho we may not be of one colour we're humans
And can live as we want if you dare
CHORUS

{ ... fade out ... }
I'm in need of some friendship today
I'm in need of some friendship today
I'm in need of some loving today

I'm Going Back To Shanna

I'm going back to Shanna

I'm going back to Shanna

I'm going back to Shanna in Shenandoah

'Way down there in Dixie

Where I spent my childhood

I'm going back to Shanna in Shenandoah

There's an old grey haired lady

Who waits for me with Shanna

There's an old grey haired lady in Shenandoah

She's my blessed mother

She's my precious mother

She's my mother dear in Shenandoah.

CHORUS:

Shenandoah -- Shenandoah

Home of the happiest times I've known

There where all my folks and kin

Lives life like it's always been

That's why I'm going back to Shenandoah

I'm going back to Shanna

I'm going back to Shanna

I'm going back to Shanna in Shenandoah

Where beneath the green green grass lies

My poor father's dead body

There 'neath the tall elms shadow in Shenandoah

CHORUS

I'm going back to Shanna

I'm going back to Shanna

I'm going back to Shanna in Shenandoah

When I get outa this prison

And I've gained back my freedom

I'm going back to Shanna in Shenandoah

I'm going back to Shanna

Who once meant love to me there

She helped make the happiest time I've known

So when I leave this prison

I'm going back to Shanna --

I'm going back to Shanna in Shenandoah

CHORUS twice

If This Is Love

If this is love which you are giving
If this is love well I'm not winning
If this is love then I'm not playing
'Cause it's clear that I am losing
Losin', losing, losing you
If this is love then you deceived me
If this is love you lied you'll agree
If this IS love I wish you'd free me
'Cause by now it's too clear to see
So Darling please just let me be
If this is love I've had my share
If this is love I can't live anywhere
If this is love 'tis all that I can bear
'Cause by now it's too hard and clear
That your love is far from being right my dear

I Get A Feeling I'm Hearing

CHORUS: *I get a feeling I'm hearing*
The sounds of goodbye
I get a feeling
You're breaking my heart
In this try
I get a feeling
You're saying that we now must part
I get a feeling
You're saying goodbye

Busy hours
Which were ours
Have now filled all your day
Busy nights,
You spend all alone
It seems each day
Short quick phone calls

In answer
Are all that I get
And a voice filled with doubtfulness
Cold distant neglect
CHORUS

Once we loved
In a way that
Was filled with passion and warmth
Once it seemed
You just couldn't
Stay long enough in my arms
Once your lips seemed
With hunger
For mine to be graced
As your worshipful brown eyes
With love looked in my face
CHORUS

Dear God Up In Heaven Above

Dear God up in Heaven above
My heart and my Soul are lonely
My voice cries ever thy name
I wait for thy coming glory
And pray that I'll meet you up there

CHORUS: *Up there (up there) Up there (up there)*
Up there where the Heavens endures
Up there (up there) Up there (up there)
To live with thee Free evermore

Dear God up in Heaven above
Smile down on a sinner like me
Reach down with thy powerful love
Grant patience forgiveness to me
While I pray I'll meet you up there
CHORUS

Dear God up in Heaven above
Near the time draws for me to come home
My heart is so weary and filled
I'm too tired to linger on here
Call me Lord to meet you up there

Up there (up there) Up there (up there)

Up there where the Heavens endures

Up there (up there) Up there (up there)

Up there free with Thee evermore

Up there free with Thee evermore

30/7/81

The Heart I Couldn't Own

(to the tune of "May You Never Be Alone Like Me" Hank Williams)

Like a ship that's tillerless in the storm

My heart's been tossed around since you've been gone

But I hoped you'll find another one

Who'd share the love I couldn't own

You have beauty unsurpassed it's true

And I'll always be a fool for you

'Cause first love should always be the only one

I'm sorry now your heart I couldn't own

I pray that God will understand

And yet smile upon our bitter land

And retain her soul when life is done

And may He bless the heart I couldn't own

The Seaman's Serenade

(to the tune of "Geisha Girl")

Have you ever heard the story
Of the men who sail the seas
Did you ever hear the seagull's wings
A-fluttering in the breeze
Do you really understand the life
Of those who ride the waves
Did you ever stop and listen to
The Seaman's Serenade

No song could ever be more sweet
Yet sad and lonely too
No person ashore could ever know
The feeling of the blue
Where everyone is like a brother
Sorrow and unknown joys they share
Yet each can tell a lone love story
Which makes him sing
The Seaman's Serenade

'Til Eternity

'Til eternity my memory will rock with love for you

'Til eternity my memory will rock with love for you

I look at weddings they cause a frown

'Cause mine was so happy 'til you put me down

Now I hate to see you far from me

For all eternity

'Til eternity my memory will rock with love for you

Won't You Please Come Back

Once you were my sweetheart

Then you went away

Once you said you loved me

Won't you come back to stay

Won't you believe I'm sorry

Won't you believe I'm sad

Won't you ease an aching heart

Won't you please come back

Once I was free and happy

Once you were sunshine gay

Once we held a future bright

But spoiled it in a day

Burning Evils Behind Me

(to the tune of "Burning Bridges")

Burning evils behind me

Things of life I care for not now

Burning evils behind me

All I want is God's forgiving love

Sold the items I worked with this morning

Tools for gambling and killing so cruel

Now they're gone and my desire is for gaining

Heavenly treasures promised by You

Sold the bars where sin we had gathered

Said goodbye to the night life I knew

And I moved to the church God's Sanctuary

There by his grace to start life anew

Burning evils behind me

Things of life I care for not now

Burning evils behind me

All I want is God's forgiving love

Sold the items I worked with this morning

Tools for gambling and killing so cruel

Now they're gone and my desire is for gaining

Heavenly treasures promised by You

Man-Made Honky Tonk Angel

I love that man-made honky tonk angel
The one who once was my true and trusty wife
I know now that I brought her eternal sorrow
And must live my lone regretful life

Yes I know now we men take too much for granted
And lay the blame on our trusty ones
But I don't care if you're a Honky tonk Angel
I'll take your part 'cause I know I made you one

I hope you'll have no regrets my Darling
When your journey on the earth is through
And I pray you'll ask God to forgive me
For I made a honky tonk angel out of you

I don't believe God made honky tonk Angels
As I said in the words of that song
No I don't believe God made honky tonk Angels
But I do believe I caused you to go wrong

Just Hold Me, Hold Me

Hold me — oh -oh Baby hold me please hold me
Oh so tightly, hold me hold me all thru the night
Hold me — okay Baby oh kiss me kiss me
Kiss me — Kiss me — with all your might
Love me — okay Baby, love me love me tonight
Hold me — Baby hold me oh so tight
Just hold me, hold me, hold me Baby hold me so tight

The feeling of your lips on mine
Is like tasting sweet sweet cherry wine
The warmth of your embrace
Brings joy to me any time or place
So Darling please just
Give me all that you can give me
Show me that our love can be so right
Take me in your Heart — Embrace me
Be mine Baby — Baby each and every night

Darling As I Write You

Darling as I write you this letter
I hope that you're thinking of me
For soon I'll be home
No more will I roam
But I'll walk you home in the Moonlight
And once more our love will be free

Don't Leave Me Now

Of all the girls I ever knew
You know it's you that I love true
Honest faithful 'til I die
Don't leave me now don't let me cry
You know you are the only one
I'll love you dear 'til life is done
Our love'll outlive the hate and lies
Don't leave me now don't make me cry
Why can't we go on this way
Living happily everyday
Waiting for the sweet by and by
Don't leave me now don't let me cry

Is It Really

Is it really your hair that makes sunshine
Is it really your tears that form rain
Is it really the touch of your lips warm on mine
Is it really your sweet breath I feel
When the sky is without sunshine
And the clouds are without rain
When the wind is gone when my lips are cold
I'll know you're his once again
But Darling there is the sunshine
And here is the joyous rain
The wind is here my lips are warm
'Cause I'm holding you close once again

I Have His Heart

I have his heart I am the one he loves

I am the one he feels unworthy of

I never meant for him to say goodbye

He's lonely now but so am I

I have his heart to do with as I please

'Cause he wants me back to relive his memories

I let him see me with another guy

Now I have his heart but still I cry

I have his heart which I've torn all apart

My jealous act was wrong right from the start

I loved him true but still I made him cry

I have his heart but still I cry

Song Lyric #68 –

A Heart And A Man

You say he's left you all alone

And you can't reason why

You're broken up because he's gone

You so often sit and cry

Your heart is full

You say that you

Just can't believe it's true

You'll never understand you say

Why he walked out on you
But baby... a heart and a man
Both are constant
Neither from sweet warmth will go
But a heart and a man
Can't be faithful
When there's nothing
To be faithful to....
He left you for some other woman
Who shares what you wouldn't give
One who knows how to be a full woman
One who likes to love and to live
No in his heart he wasn't fickle
But the truth is you didn't respond
So he's left now to live life a little
With a woman that he can count on
Maybe one day you will meet love
Love that is shared also by you
Then you'll find a man e'er near love
As you respond to all he may do
You will find then that you are a woman
Nothing greater in life could you be
When that happens then no other woman
Will see the emptiness she saw in me.

I'm Wasting My Life

I'm wasting my life on this ship all alone

At nights I dream of my lost love at home

I can picture her there

With her eyes oh so blue

And I wonder how could I ever be untrue

All my life was worth living

With her by my side

My prayers and hopes

To make her my bride

I cheated on her in some little way

Now I will regret it 'til my last day

She was my little girl

I was her only boy

Sharing together our troubles and joys

We both loved each other

Tho quarrels would come

I'd be soon forgiven

As I took her home

My Margaret

(to the tune of "Fraulein")

I was born near the water

Loved an old Scotsman's daughter

Who came to live in the West

I still have the ring I bought her

'Cause I loved her and no other

My Margaret and her warm caress

Oh — Margaret I loved thee

And wanted you only

But this you just couldn't realize

For the day that you told me

That you didn't want me

I left my home with teardrops in my eyes

Of late my memory wanders

While my broken heart ponders

Of her blue eyes and rich golden hair

And I wonder if out yonder

My Margaret remembers

The sorrow and grief she made me bear

You're Not Fool No 1

You're not fool No 1

Nor fool No 2

No other girls has been fooled this is true

So you are wrong

The number is very very small

And you'll never be fooled

I love you best of all

I would be so happy

To have you back again

If you will just promise

That at the old road's end

You'll be near tho a false love

My heart tries to call

And you'll never be fooled

I love you most of all

It's Over It's Finished It's Past

It's over it's finished it's past

My days of worry are now at an end

My nights of being without a friend

My times alone are over at last

No more do I sit alone and blue

No longer need I wait and cry

No longer pray for time to go by

No longer dream each night of you
You've taken away my hopes I know
You've spoilt all that I desired
You've made my body old and tired
You've filled my very soul with sorrow
I've tried to live without you
I've tried my best you to forget
To drown my dreams and regrets
To lose my memories of you
But alas I've found that time is thine
No longer can I stay away
From the one who fills my everyday
With thoughts of warmth and sunshine
So brightly did you grow within
That time cannot erase the glow
Of times I spent and days I know
Could be mine if you were mine again
So once more to you I return
Seeking the peace for which I yearn
Looking once more at my Island home
Dreaming anew the dreams I've learned
Can be fulfilled with you
Oh land of peace and beauty free
With soft white coral sands
You mean more than the world to me
You My Island home Cayman

I Know That I Won't Forget You

I know that I won't forget you

'Cause my love for you is too strong

You may not love me now

Tho I still love you

In my memories of you

Our love lingers on

I know you will find fond tomorrows

In the arms of a love kind and true

And even tho you are gone

Here in my heart you're my own

And I know I won't forget you

I know I'll never forget you

"No matter what new loves I find

You'll forever remain

The wants of my pains

And no other can take 'way what's mine

My heart my life and my love too

Will linger in memories of you

And I pray that you'll be

As happy as you one time made me

For my Darling I'll never forget you

It's A Strange Strange World

It's a strange strange world we live in Brother Mack

It's a strange strange world we live in that's a fact

It's a strange strange world we live in Brother Mack

It's a strange strange world -- be you white or black

Some people feel that life's unreal

And are content with what they've got

Other people feel that it's too real

And these people want the lot

Some people think to laugh and sing

While others have to cry

They've got it made by taking everything

From those they pass by ——

Some believe they're better 'cause of looks

Some feel superior 'cause of books

Some think their colour makes them right

Others think money gives a light

Some starve while others they grow fat

There are slaves 'cause some like it like that

I don't care who you are — it's a fact

Regardless if you are white or black

It's a strange strange world we live in —

Isn't it Brother Mack?

I Was Living Oh So Happy

I was living oh so happy

In my little Island home

Not a worry, want or sorrow

Did I realize or know

But I got thinking of someplace

Where I'd not been across the seas

Three years ago I came (to this place) here

And it's made a wreck of me

My days are so hard and lonely

My nights cold, dreary and long

My life here without you, only

Drags my will to live to the ground

I've known want, worry, sorrow

I've felt pangs of hunger, and of pain

And if I could go back home

No more would I roam

To these cold and lonely places e'er again

The people like machinery, struggle

In this unfeeling place to live

They live all alone but in a muddle

Like rats on a garbage hill

Each day is like the other

For God respect has long fallen down

The idea is not to help each other

But to step on those upon the ground

Their lives are so empty and so bitter

As earths vain pleasures they pursue

And as you stay on soon like a curse

You start to be like them too

And soon find that you

Are getting each and every day much worse

Don't Give Me Up

Love me when I'm happy

Love me when I'm not gay

Love me like you did before

Both lifelong night and day

Don't give me up ... don't give me up

Love me in the morning

Love me in the night

Love me if you even think

It's a little far from right

Hold me baby, squeeze me

Cuddle up real tight

Don't give me up ... don't give me up

It's Only A Letter From Home

I was working on the sea many miles from home

That day the captain called me up to his room alone

He handed me a letter saying "this is for you son"

I opened it, He asked what it contained

I said "Sir my work here is done

'Cause it's only a letter from home sweet home

From friends away in my old home town

From wife from Mother Dad sister and brothers

Saying son please come back to your own

Babe sister is whispering a prayer tonight

To guide you out thereon the sea

She's praying to God in the heavens above

Please send BOBO back safe home to me

That is all my captain" I cried

I'm heading back home you understand

With a tear in his eye he said to me son

Won't you read me your letter again

"Why it's only a letter from home sweet home

From friends away in my old home town

From wife from Mother Dad sister and brothers

Saying son please come back to your own

Babe sister is whispering a prayer tonight

To guide you out there on the sea

She's praying to God in the heavens above

Please send BOBO back safe home to me
That is all my captain" I cried
I'm heading back home you understand
With a tear in his eye he said to me son
Won't you read me your letter again

The Heart Loves

The Heart it loves a short while
If it can't have its way
Today it swears forevermore
Tomorrow goes on its way
Returns again sometimes to see
If prehaps its ways can win
If not it moves so swiftly by
Somewhere else to try again
For life and love are bargains
And each is content to go
To brighten up a bidders world
'Til that one's outbid also
Then once more for a higher bid
Content it'll rest it seems
Unless some bidder offers more
In exchange for a few dreams

I've So Oft Sat And Wondered

I've so oft sat and wondered why

The Sun and moon doth shine

So faithfully and pleasantly

Upon these sins like mine

'Til one day I sat alone

And in a book I read

The words which by our God was given

To twelve men that he led

AND HE SAID ****

Our Father

not yours, not mine, not theirs, by far, but ours alone, like

one our own who knows

Who art in Heaven

removed from all our sins and woes to watch apart with

loving heart and still forgive us all

Hallowed be thy name

lest we forget that thou art holy and deserves esteem

Thy kingdom come

we hope and pray that life with thee we'll share

Thy will be done

for the will of man has brought us pain and shame

On Earth

the dwelling place you gave, where thy loving Son we

murdered

As it is in Heaven

So may our future lives be free and pleasant

While we live here

Give us this day

the strength we need, the patience and the wisdom

To ever have ambition for

Our daily bread

lest we feel it's ours just for the taking

And forgive us our debts

Lord we humbly pray for all of our gross misdemeanors

As we forgive our debtors

That in thy footsteps we may walk in love, respect

and understanding of and for our brothers

Lead us not

where thou would have us stray away from dangers

Into temptation

such as the devil tries to draw us

Deliver us

this day and next and all our days hereafter

From Evil

and our sinful ways that we may live and dwell forever

in the home where thou hast prepared with the shed blood

of thy Son

For Christ's sake so be it evermore may all our joys and

sorrows be stepping stones for our bright tomorrows

When I Feel Alone And Downhearted

When I feel alone and downhearted

When my memories of you grow dim

When I recall that sad night we parted

'Cause I saw you there love with him

Then my old heartaches renew love

And my fondest memories recall

For I know now you'll ever be my love

So come back to me my one and all

Why do we pretend we don't care dear

Why do we act so foolishly

Why do we try to hurt each other

'Stead of loving strong and tenderly

Now my acting days are over

As my heart to you loud calls out

Let's not cause heartaches to linger

Let us live and find what loves about

So come to me dear in the morning

Or come when midsun is high

Or come at the strokes of midnight

I'll be waiting here for a new try

Our love deserves a start anew

Our life deserves memories forever

You deserve a love that's true

And I long to be worthy to deserve you

Just Like Heaven Cayman Islands

(to the tune of "Country Roads" by John Denver)

Just like heaven
Cayman Islands —
Coral Shorelines
Blue Caribbean waters
Our lands are older
Older yet than we
Younger in their beauty   ---
Resting in our Seas

CHORUS: **Trade winds blow**
Take me home
To the Isles —
I love so
Cayman Islands
West Indian Sunshine
Take me home
Oh Trade winds blow

All my memories
Harbour 'round her
Dreams of moonlight
On calm cool waters
Takes my thoughts and
Takes my yearnings
To my home where
I'll soon be returning
{repeat CHORUS}

Ask And You Shall Be Given

Ask and you shall be given
Seek and you shall find
Knock and it shall be opened
The love in this heart of mine
Be to your brothers loving
Your neighbours honest and true
Each with each other loving
These are his words to you

You want peace, peace, peace and happiness
You want joy, joy, joy and contented bliss
You want love, love, love and a warm caress
Follow my teachings and be assured of this
There's a whole lot to living
This I'm sure you'll see
There's many a gross misgiving
Known to you and me
But hold your head up highly
Look steadfast to the sky
And the woes of the world will go quickly
From the thoughts of you and I

And at last when life is ended
And our journey here is through
You will need not be offended
By what others say or do
We'll live together forever
In that heavenly bliss above
Where our days they will end never
Living warm in each other's love

I Love the Way It Feels

I love the way it feels
To hold a baby in my arms
And feel their racing heart go calm
And see their smile contentedly
As safe secure it's plain they feel
I love the way it feels.

I love the way it feels
To help a child at work or play
And watch their look of wonderment
As we do something new to them
Which is old to me from yesterday
I love the way it feels.

I love the way it feels
And I can still be part of it
When I can with an adult blend
And light their load along the way
Or ease the pain of life they bear
With word or deed or smile as friend
I love the way it feels.

I love the way it feels
To hold a woman in my arms
And still her doubtful tremblings
I love the way it feels
To ease her fears caress her skin
Feel lips warm pressed to mine give in
Feel rubber form where knees have been
And hear her softly whispering
"I love the way it feels".

I love the way it feels
To be alive and be a man
To be a part of some great plan
Which fulfills what's inside of me
And claims my spot in history
Leaving my mark in my own clan
To show I've lived and loved as man
And been loved too oh it's so grand
I love the way it feels   Yes, I love the way it feels.   300693-1

The Old Churchyard

(to the tune of "Green Green Grass of Home")

The old churchyard looks the same
As when a child I first played there
And there's the headstones for my mother and father
Down that lane I walked and left my family
Home and church and all God's mercies
When I despised the Christian ways at home
The old bell still tolls clearly
Tho the padre now is gone
And the gospel organ sounds as ever before
The voice of sacred music fills the air
Spreading God's love everywhere
Comforting the Christian folks at home
Oh they all came to see me
Kneeling there where I'll e'er be
Asking forgiveness from the God
That I'd let down
Then I awake and look around me
The prison of sin no more surrounds me
Then I realize me my God forgave once more
And there's the church with the sad old padre
Who's promised now in God's way to lead me
And I'll never despise the Christian ways no more
Yes they'll all come to hear me
Telling how from sin God saved me
As I spread His love
Among the Christian folks at home

My Mama Sang Gospel Chorus

When I was just a little teeny baby
My Mama sang gospel chorus to me
Telling me of Jesus and a heavenly home
When I was just a little teeny baby
My Mama sang Gospel chorus to me
Telling me of Jesus and a heavenly home
How Jesus was first begotten
How by the world He was forsaken
When He told them of a heavenly home
How on a cross He was crucified
Despised forsaken and denied
'Cause He told them of, of a heavenly home
He came to tell them of a heavenly home
He came to tell them of a home a home
Where sorrow want and pain
Will never be known
Yes He told them of a heavenly home
He came He lived and He died
That our soul would all be sanctified
And He could take us to that heavenly home
When my Jesus started talking
Of how man's sins could be forgiven
By God there on the heavenly throne
When my Jesus started talking
Angels chorus started singing
"How great Thou art"
Around the heavenly throne

It's Late And I'm Growing Tired

It's late and I'm growing tired

I've worked and tried to do my best

To live and let those I live with

Enjoy this life to its fullest

I've looked afar across land and sea

For joy of life and peace of mind

But through this life it seems to me

These two things I will never find

And so once more to you I turn

In hopes of finding while I can

The things for which my heart does yearn

The things you've promised unto man

The joys of life before I die

The peace of mind that passed me by

The knowledge sweet of an easy mind

The sweet release from these sins of mine

The feeling of being one -- your own

The fulfillments I have never known

The hopes of life beyond the grave

The answer once to all my prayers

The joy the peace the full surrender

To your will and majesty forever

The rich rewards I do crave after

Yes it's so late and I'm growing tired

But before I pass along my way

Lend me a hand and Lord an ear

Listen once more as to you I pray

"Our Father, which art in Heaven

Hallowed be thy name

Thy kingdom come thy will be done

On Earth as it is in Heaven

Give us this day our daily bread

And forgive us our debts

As we forgive our debtors

And lead us not into temptation

But deliver us from evil

For Thine is the kingdom

And the Power and the Glory

Forever and ever more"

What Is Youth

What is youth

A burning fire

What is a woman

Ice and desire

A rose will bloom

It then will fade

So does youth

So does the fairest maid

He Is There In My Heart

He is there in my heart

Now and forever

And my life got its start

When I made Him mine

He had lived been crucified

Come from Heaven and died

While no one noticed

That the million guitars

Played love songs

Telling of hearts soon to be broken

But a few such as you

To the Saviour so true

Spread the good news far

Reaching my heart with love

Of a home up above

With my Lord everafter

Now I own all the stars

Where celestial guitars play God's love songs

And I'm so proud it is true

I hope you'll join us too

That He'll always be there

In your heart

God Will Take Care Of You

God will take care of you while we're apart
You'll walk by His precious side
He'll be your comfort wherever thou art
For by His promise He will abide
You'll never walk in dark shadows alone
You'll never know more of pain or of fear
You'll feed in green pastures with Jesus alone
For by His promises He'll lead you there

WHY **** WHY **** WHY
'Cause "You have heard my voice" He said
"And you have kept my Word and
You have befriended your fellowman"
Yes you've brought joy to Earth

In the book of ages written
With the seal of God above
He promises you'll never be smitten
If you but keep His words of love
He gives us all the little things
With which our lives to live
He protects us from the greatest fiends
If to Him our life we'll just give

In this world such as we know
He's placed the challenges wild
For those who from His ways may go
To confuse in all their wiles

Man too but a creature He has made
With forms like beasts of the wild
Like the lowly beasts to which He said
We'll be tamed by the hands of a child

When God Smiles Down On Us

The sun gets up and lights the dawn
When God smiles down on us
The rain fell from the sky this morn
When God smiled down on us
The sea is calm the rivers flow
The mountains stay the trees still grow
As man tries farther from God to go
While God smiles down on us

The Sun was darkened it gave no light
When God frowned down on us
The rains fell in floods both day and night
When God frowned down on us

The seas were rough the rivers wild
The mountains quaked the trees turned fire
But man he returned not from his mire
'Cause God frowned down on us

One day alas the Sun shall fall
When God gets mad at us
The waters will be no more at all
When God gets mad at us
The seas shall flee the rivers dry
The mountains fall the trees bare lie
And man will find no place to hide
When God gets mad at us

Then the new Sun it will shine again
When God lives here with us
We'll know no sorrow want or pain
When God lives here with us
The water trees and mountains tall
Will be renewed in splendour all
And there'll only be men that heard the call
When God lives here with us

Forgive Me For Being The One

(to the tune of "When I Walk The Last Mile")

Forgive me for being the one
Whose name caused you shame
I made the mistake for which you now pay
I've travelled the long road of life
I've reached my last mile
I had hoped to be worthy of you,
As you came down an aisle
Police came for me at eight
To take me away
I spent just four days in their jail
But my life without you will fail
For you fled when the going got rough
I didn't think that you would
I thought your love strong enough
I tried all I could
Now each of us go on our ways
Both living a lie
A prison term brought on ourselves
Until we shall die
Don't cry over me now I'm gone
Tho I'll cry for you
But if you ever escape from your cell
Please come free me too

The Lord Is My Shepherd

The Lord is my shepherd,

He cares for me as tho I was a helpless lamb

I shall not want,

Whatsoever I need in this life

He in His generous goodness supplies

He maketh me to lay down in green pastures,

Wheresoever I go I'll rest in Peace and comfort

secure under His protection

He leadeth me besides the still waters,

My rough and stormy days He makes smooth

By His love, **He restoreth my Soul**

When life gets me down just knowing of Him

refreshes and starts me anew

He leadeth me in the paths of righteousness

In this sinful sin-filled world of temptations

He guides me along

the roads whereby I will avoid

becoming one of the crowd

For His names Sake

Why does He do all this?

Because His own Son died that I might live

and He lends His helping hand whenever I stumble

Yea, tho I walk thru the valley of the shadow of death,

At times my life will take me to evil places

as a test of my love

and endurances but **I will fear no evil,**

Still no matter where I go

I am never fearful of the surrounding

evils and dangers of life

For Thou art with me,

Yes, He is there besides me in all and through all

Thy Rod and Thy Staff they comfort me,

His strength love and helpful guidance

will always be there to comfort

and reassure me

Thou preparest a table before me

When I am hungered or alone

He joins me at a table either mentally

or materially visible which is fit for a king to sit at

In the presence of mine enemies,

I need not seek vengeance on any

who doeth me wrong as He better shows

them by His assistance to me that I am His child

and invulnerable to them

Thou annointest my head with oil,

In His generosity He provides me with all I need

yet leaves the finals to me to obtain thru my efforts

as He fills my head with ideas to use

My cup runneth over,

By His filling my mind with worthy ideas and by my working

them as He instructs

I am rewarded far beyond my wildest imaginations

Surely goodness and mercy shall follow me,

All bad that befalls me amounts to nothing

in comparison to the Peace Joy and Happiness

He gives me through my darkest sorrows

All the days of my life,

These things He continues to give freely

as long as He sees fit to let me remain in this evil world

And I shall dwell in the house of the Lord forever,

Then on that beautiful day when He shall decide that my

short journey of endurance has been a success

He gives me His divine promise that I

thereafter shall live with Him in His Heavenly mansions

where evil never enters, sorrow is unknown,

He will be besides me always and best of all

Time shall have no end Amen...Amen...Amen

And He Promises by His Divine Unbreakable word

"No Weapon formed against You Shall Prosper"

As God's Sun Was Slowly Sinking

As God's Sun was slowly sinking
O'er the hills the seas and plains
There laid upon my mind a melody
And it was such a sweet refrain ——— of

CHORUS: *Days of the still waters*
When I walked with the Lord
To nights on green pastures
In the fold of my God
Oh my cup it overfloweth
With riches aye full store
Of the blessedness of contentment
Of which I know now no more ———

As the treetops and the mountains
Did their splendour all forsake
For the dark watch of the nighttime
My thoughts went back with an ache —— For

CHORUS

And the clouds they did get blacker
And the sea 'twas not so calm
And I longed to return there
Where I was safe secure from harm ———in

Oh my soul is now the hilltops

And my sins are all the clouds

Which covers o'er the hills splendour

Of which I once was proud ——— in

CHORUS

But beyond that far horizon

Where my God's face now has gone

One day I'll journey on to meet Him

And once more live with my Lord ——— in

CHORUS

Then my soul it shall lie rested

And I'll find 'gain peace of mind

When I return to the fold great

Of that Shepherd so divine ——— living

CHORUS

Moon Up Above

Moon up above, is it the stars,

or clouds, or ripples on the sea

Is it the birds in the air,

Or the Sun — that keeps you company?

Moon up above, do you hold the world in your arms

Don't you realize the hearts you've broken

With your soft sweet charms?

Moon, do you really care or understand

Do you rejoice as in your light

Young lovers hold each other's hand?

Moon up above, if only you could speak

Or let me know somehow

The real meaning of Beauty

Peace, Joy and true love

Don't you think I would be more happy then

If I could explain these things

To the hard hearts of men

Oh Moon, we could have a world so full of Peace

If only you could speak —

Or I could understand

The words your heart is longing to release

Thank God His Love Has Lifted Me

(to the tune of "May You Never Be Alone Like Me")

Like a bird that's lost its mate in flight

I was alone and living my sinful life

Like a piece of driftwood on the sea

But thank God His love has lifted me

I gave up my God and left His fold

Thinking life's treasures I would rather hold

'Til to worldly gain I'd lost my soul

But thank God His love has made me whole

In the Bible God's own word I read

How He died and of the life He led

How on the cross He suffered in my stead

Thank God He forgives us all He said

So sinner friend 'tis time like me you find

The peace and fullness you now leave behind

Make God yours just like I made him mine

And thank God His love is true divine

"Thank God His love has lifted me

From the burdens of sin He set me free

He paid the price I owed on Calvary

Thank God His love has lifted me"

Making Love And Passion

(Making love may sound so beautiful

But only Passion can satisfy)

Making love's a way, we choose to say,

To the world, what we would do,

An outward way, to write, and say,

What goes on between us two,

It's a norm, to hide, feelings behind,

While the world, looks in our eye

"Making love may sound so beautiful,

But only Passion can satisfy"

Making love's a thing, that dreamers dream,

Of tender words, and looks and touch,

Making love's a feeling left half-filled,

Careful not, to take too much,

It's the thing, that causes us to let,

All our fantasies pass us by

"Making love may sound so beautiful,

But only Passion can satisfy"

Making love's o-kay, while we're out

And I can't hold you tight,

But don't be put off, if I whisper rough,

Forbidden words, to you at night,

For when the world has left us,

You my passions multiply,

"Making love may sound so beautiful,

But only passion can satisfy"

Making love is soft, and warm, and dry,

And it lasts for just a while,

But passion is rough, hard, hot and wet

Leaves you breathless a long time,

With tangled sheets 'n' shaking limbs

For more desperately you'll try

'Cause making Love may sound so beautiful,

But only Passion can satisfy

Making love may sound so beautiful

But only Passion can satisfy

Yes making love may sound so beautiful

Ahhh.....But... only passion can satisfy

I Am Cold

Cold,

What is cold

I am cold

I am without warmth

I am alone with no heart

No heat

No fire

No love

No desire to live on

I am cold

I am cold

I am like winters wind

Like fresh fallen snow

Like grass waiting still to grow

When winter's gone

When snow is past

When spring comes on anew

I am cold

I am cold

Like lost birds flying

Like a child lone straying

Like the freezing rain falling

Such as icicles

Such as icy topped lakes

Such as white topped mountains

Cold

I am cold

I am cold

Yes but I am cold so cold

Only because

I have lost your warmth

Go Get Her

Go get her go get her go get her
What should you do
When there is a girl
And you know that she truly loves you
Go get her, go get her, go get her
You can if you want to
You can if you want to
What should you do
When her parents stand in the way
Yet you know in your heart
That her love it lives on
Go get her, go get her, go get her
You can if you want to
You can if you try
Why try pretending with someone new
It can't be the same when she's meant for you
What should you do to let her parents realize
She'll love you forever as she does now
Go get her, go get her, go get her
I've heard that before
Don't tell me anymore
I'm leaving to find her
I'll get her somehow
I'm leaving to find her
To get her somehow
I'm leaving to find her
So goodbye for now

Take This Sorrow From My Heart

(Roughly the tune of "Help Me Make It Through The Night")

Take this sorrow from my heart

Let your love live there instead

Give my life a brand new start

Keep me love from feeling dead

Come and befriend me one time

Life is short let's make it right

Tho you may ne'ermore be mine

Be a friend to me tonight

I don't know what's right or wrong

I am just a lonely man

But just once to hold you tight

'Twould fulfill my every plan

Yesterday I was sad it's gone

Tomorrow you may be out of sight

Let's not waste then all our time

Be a friend to me tonight.

<u>Love Is</u> -- (An Action Poem)

Love is a two way street ---

A two way street ---

My love is a two way street ---

A street ---

A street of giving and sharing

As well as taking

A street of needing and waiting

And not sporadic pretending

Love is a two way street

A two way street

Love is a two way street

So don't expect me

Don't expect me day after day

Don't expect me day after day

To sit

To sit and wait and wait

And wait and wait for nothing

Don't expect me to sit and wait

And don't expect me ----Night after night

I say, don't expect me night after night

To lay -- and want -- and need

Don't expect me to lay and want and need

Don't expect me to lay and want and need

The affections you never give

Don't expect me ---

Don't expect me to love

Don't expect me to love to love unending

Don't expect me to love unending

While you give nothing in return

Don't expect me to sit -- or lay -- or wait --

Or need for love

For love is a two way street

A two way street

A street of giving, giving and sharing

A street of loving and caring

Love is a two way street...

Love is a two way street, a two way street

Nothing more or less, just a damn two way street

Don't expect me to react to your charms

Don't expect me to react to your charms

Don't don't expect me to react to charms

Charms held back, charms favour traded

Charms given once twice a month

Charms given when you feel a need

Charms given when you have a want

Charms given in meager measure

Given only at your selfish whim

No, don't expect me to react to your charms

Don't expect me to react

My love is a two way street

My love is a two way street

Like a pipe flowing full without a valve

Like a free wind on all blowing

Like laughter of real joy and happiness

Like innocence of a new born babe

My love is a two way street

My love is a two way street

My love is a two way street

Waiting --- waiting

Waiting for you to walk into

Don't expect me to stifle

Don't expect me to stifle my love

Don't expect me to stifle my love

Then let it flow at your beck and call

Don't expect me to bottle up

Don't expect me to bottle up for weeks

Don't expect me to bottle up for weeks alone

Awaiting the day or two you feel to love

My love is a two way street

Love is a two way street

Love is a two way street

And if you walk it

If you walk it, If you walk it freely

If you walk it frequently

If you walk it, if you walk it daily
If you walk it conscientiously
You will find me, you will find me
You will always find me
Waiting -- waiting patiently there
You will find me there
You will always and forever
Find me there
'Cause love is a two way street
Love is a two way street
Love is a two way street
And I survive knowing this
I survived believing this
I survive because of this
I survive because love is my existence
Love is my life's sustenance
Love is my breath, my life, my soul
And so I seek it and I share it
For love, my love, my love is a two way street
My love is a two way street
My love is an open two way street
Yes my love is a two way street
Come walk up it, come walk up it
Come walk it and share it with me.

Let Me Tell YOU An Old Story

Let me tell you an old story

Of my youths time of glory

When I lived yet in my little island home

We heard the many tales and stories

Of the Klan and their racist history

'Til one day my Daddy came back home

He'd been away for most two years

On the sea he toiled thru without fears

So when he heard the many tales of woe begone

My Daddy, He called us to his side

And beaming full of Cayman Island pride

He gave up the answer to the trouble of the Klan

Here in our little island of Cayman

Even tho through Slavery aches we did go

We have never been so beaten

As to let our pride be so broken

That now free men we'll e'er let it go

So my Son go tell your Brother

Uncle, Aunt, Sister and friend

That it's time long past and we swear

No More, no more "Neva, Neva a'gin"

So when you try to bring we

Hate, Prejudice and Bigotry

Is our ways you'll find here with me

As we teach you a few things

Things that'll forever revenge for times past

"For here in our Island there's no Ghost,

There's no Duppy and no sheeted klansman ever

Cause we have an answer here for one and all"

If you try to push us down

We stand upon your shoulder

And we stay there 'til you give up or you fall

And our younger or lil ones too

Give such a shoe-fitting there to you

That you give us trouble no no Neva-more

Then comes the Sheeted Ghost well well well

These things we fight in cane-fields long time gone

So with same stick and rock and machete

We cut them up again so fast

That British Man-O-Wars can't find them

And at times of night the sheeted too they try

Again we there waiting for them

With many various kinds of shooting guns

'Til such as bother us find they canna' win a fight

And they leave us happy in our Island homes

Nov 16th, 2012

For You Are My Love

My heart is like a headless arrow
speeding pointlessly towards an ungiving target
thereat to strike against and fall away from to
rest lonely and alone upon the ground
by the target's feet

My love is like a smooth river stone waiting
cold and alone as feelingless as the river crashes
ever onwards over it unaware of its existence
and leaving not so much as a bit of moss behind

My life is like the far beyond of heavenly
expanse waiting cold and empty and forlorn
while the planets each revolve uncaringly
nearby yet never sharing their warmth

My hopes are like dewdrops upon a Summer's
morning grass just a diamonds glitter of
nothingness which is dashed away each time a
little warmth of the Summer's Sun falls upon them

My dreams are like wisps of clouds forming a
thousand myriad shapes and colours in the dawn
and in the dusklight yet never retaining
either when the Sun moves on

My desires are like songs soft and sweet upon
an evening breeze which drifts out to some
waiting ear but once heard passes on out and
ever outwards into empty space

But you (NAME) my Love, are the Sun which
lends life to my empty loneliness, colour to my
colourless skies and myriad clouds, warmth to
my hopes my dreams my desires.

You are the one who puts a point into my pointless
life and causes green fields to grow upon my
smooth and barren grounds.

You are the light, the expanse, the cause, the
well-being, the joy and the happiness of my
otherwise drab and seemingly empty life

For you (NAME) are my Love.............

Believe Me

There is a LIE in the middle of "BeLIEve"

Believe me – Believe me

If you were mine you'd never know a heartache

Believe me – Believe me

If you were mine I'd never let you cry

Believe me I'd spend my life just for you

If you were mine

Believe me – Believe me – Believe me

There'd never be goodbye

<he/she said>

CHORUS:

Believe me, Believe me, Believe me

'Twas not a word of truth within it

Because in the middle of Believe

There is nothing but a "LIE"

Believe me, Believe me, Believe me

'Twas not a word of truth within it

Except in the middle of Believe

There is nothing just a "LIE"

Tho I recall each tender promise given

Tho I believed each word that now makes me cry

Tho I took to heart so deep all I was promised

For I could not see within Believe

There was nothing but a LIE

<he/she said>

CHORUS

Now he/she is gone and alone again I'm crying

Just like I did before her/his love came by

Before I looked so deeply at Believing

And saw within it held just this truth

Nothing but a "LIE"

<he/she said>

In the middle of Believe

There is nothing but a "LIE"

In the middle of Believe

There is nothing but a "LIE"

In the middle of Believe

There is nothing but a "LIE"

Song Lyric #67 --

<u>Mr. President</u>

(To the tune of Blue Velvet Band)

The White House

Washington, D. C., U.S.A.

Dear Mr. President,

You tore up our home when he left me

On your orders he flew 'cross the seas

Now you've sent me three Vietnam Medals

But here Sir, they're no good to me.

So... Golden... Bronzed and Silvered

A packet to you I return

May they help to bring you forgiveness

May they help Sir your soul not to burn

My life was once quite contented

My children a Daddy once knew

Now we live in the ghetto on welfare

And yes Sir it's all 'cause of you.

You've taken our men by the thousand

To fight in a strange foreign land

Still at home we know of no freedom

And for their lives you send a Blue Velvet Band...

Out Of My Life Like A Candle

Out of my life like a candle
Heaving my love dreams aside
Coldly you left me a-drifting
Heart broke and wretched inside
I who had loved and so needed
Cared for and wanted you too
Kicked like an old empty vessel
Yearning yet drifting from you
Into the abyss of nothing
Leaving behind all my plans
Over the deep end of hurting
Visions of you and some man
Ever I'll keep searching and loving
Dark tho my pathways may seem
You someday somewhere in future
Out of nowhere to me will beam
Until that moment my prayer love
Silent will keep just that you
Out there will find true happiness
Much that it hurts losing you

April 1977

Satisfied Woman

Oh oh no no and

There's nothing makes a man

Walk like a man

Like his satisfied woman

And there's nothing makes a man

Talk like a man

Like his satisfied woman

And nothing makes a man

Feel like a man

Like his satisfied woman

And oh oh woman you

You look like a satisfied woman

Yes yes woman woman you

You act like a satisfied woman

Wo wo wo woman you you speak

Like a satisfied woman

And I can walk and talk and feel

And I can shout like a man for real

Yea shout like a man for real

For you, you, you're my my satisfied woman

I, Dear Lord, Am Just A Sinner

I, Dear Lord, am just a sinner

Struggling thru this life of woe

Wondering which road is the right one

And up which course I ought to go

No wise and shrewd experienced traveler

I must but go where I feel right

So reach thee down and guide my footsteps

That I'll be led by thy life's light

Take hold of me my Precious Saviour

My way so long has wayward been

I know not now if I am walking

In paths to thee or into sin

You know my life has not been easy

Yet you have made each burden light

And been my strength and inspiration

My friend and guide thru darkest night

So Jesus Jesus heavenly Saviour

You who once my sins forgave

Reach down reclaim your wayward traveler

And free me from this life of shame

Give me again thy joy of living

Show me thy love like in times past

Take me to thee as thine forever

Where in eternal Peace I'll rest at last

Let Me Sing The Glad Praises Again

CHORUS:
Let me sing the glad praises again
The ones with the joyous refrain
Which have lifted my soul
And had made me once whole
Let me sing Jesus' praises again

Once I sang songs of his wonder
Once I spoke words of his love
Once I walked in the ways he exampled
As I reached for his home up above

Once my life was joy filled with meaning
Once my steps along life's ways were light
Once my heart sang as I was believing
That his way was the way that was right

Now I struggle and fight for survival
Now I know hate and fear most everywhere
Now no peace wake or sleep do I find
Since I no longer go to him daily in prayer

Don'tcha Tell Me

CHORUS:

Now don'tcha tell me

I have no Father

Now don'tcha tell me

I have no Lord

Now don'tcha tell me

I have no Saviour

And don'tcha tell me

There is no God

I was drifting, in a sea of sorrow

Lost and headed for a land of fire

When a firm hand fell, upon my shoulder

And the gentle strength of love, lifted me from the mire

When my trials and tribulations,

So heavy felt I could not stand

My load was lifted my eyes saw clearly,

From the moment that I placed my life fully in his hands

For I've been saved by his tender mercies

I've been cleansed by his precious blood

I've been forgiven through the death he suffered

And it's written, yes it's written in His Holy Word

I Am Just A Ferry Boat

I am just a ferry boat
On the turbulent sea of life
Drifting ever back and forth
Between two distant ports
I am just a ferry boat
Taking peoples on their way
Never getting to a home
Nor coming in a port to stay
Times my sides are full and free
Times my insides are bare
Times I drift on placid tide
Times there's turmoil everywhere
Deep within my engines moan
Sounds like peals of laughter
But 'tis only those nearby
Understands the strain it's under
Hit a port for short a time
Feel my spirit lifting
Only to 'gain be cut free
Once more my ports a-shifting
Stuck it seems to ever be
Just a drifting ferry boat
I am just a ferry boat
On the turbulent sea of life
Drifting ever back and forth
Between two distant ports

I'm Putting It All Together

I'm putting it all together
While you keep pulling it apart
Our life our love our marriage
What's wrong where did it start
You once said that you loved me
You once cared back at the start
Now I'm putting it all together
While you keep pulling it all apart

I'm putting it all together
You keep pulling it all apart
Lonely nights spent cold beside you
Lonely days near yet apart
You keep avoiding my advances
When you I try to reach sweetheart
I'm putting it all together
You keep pulling it all apart

I'm still putting it all together
You're thru pulling it all apart
I'll try somehow to salvage
What's left now of my heart
If you need again my loving
Come on here and we can start
By putting back all together
The love you pulled so all apart

Tear Me -- That's What I Call Me

Tear me -- That's what I call me

Tear me -- You've made me be

Tear me -- They just keep falling

Falling, falling from old Tear me.

Tear me -- My heart's asunder

Tear me -- I walk a loner

Tear me -- In streamlike showers

Wet stays the eyes of Tear me.

Tear me -- Once happy loving

Tear me -- Now sick empty feeling

Tear me -- Red eyed from weeping

Since you turned away from Tear me.

Tear me -- Can't you hear me calling

Tear me -- Why don't ya come back darling

Tear me -- I will return to smiling

Just to have you living near Tear me.

Touch Me

Touch me

Oh touch me lightly

And show me a better way

Lead me

But lead me straightly

'Long life's bitter dark highway

Show me

Please show me clearly

A new outlook at life

Help me

Won't you help me early

To end this hate and strife

You are the key to my heaven

The lock so safe on my door

Your ways project a beginning

One I've never seen before

Only with your hand and help strong

Will I be led on my way

With your touch alone I go along

Dear Lord through another day

<u>Other Collections By This Author:</u>

A Poet's Ebb And Flow

. . . and Touches Of Nature

Inside A Heart

Judge Me Not Without A Trial

Legends, Lives & Loves Along the Inside Passage

Love... Life's Illusive Zenith

Love's Reflections

Love's Refuge and Sonnets

Only Children Of The Universe Are We

Step Scenes Of Life

That We Too Free May Live

~ ~

For more information go to:

w w w . d n c s i t e . c a

~ ~

www.ingramcontent.com/pod-product-compliance
Lightning Source LLC
Chambersburg PA
CBHW021345090426
42742CB00008B/748